THE HAUNTINGS

Jeffrey Loffman lives in a village outside Sandwich in Kent. He spent his childhood in London and grew up in Yorkshire, obtaining a degree at Hull University.

His first book, *Breath-Taking: A Geography* was published by Lapwing in 2016.

The Hauntings

Jeffrey Loffman

Valley Press

First published in 2023 by Valley Press
Woodend, The Crescent, Scarborough, YO11 2PW
www.valleypressuk.com

ISBN 978-1-915606-06-8
Cat. no. VP0213

Copyright © Jeffrey Loffman 2023

The right of Jeffrey Loffman to be identified as the
author of this work has been asserted in accordance with
the Copyright, Designs and Patents Act 1988.

All rights reserved. No part of this publication may be
reproduced, stored in or introduced into a retrieval system,
or transmitted in any form, by any means (electronic,
mechanical, photocopying, recording or otherwise) without
prior written permission from the rights holders.

A CIP record for this book is available from the British Library.

Cover, text design and edited by Peter Barnfather.

Cover artwork: Franz Marc, 'The Fate of the Animals'
(1913), in Kunstmuseum Basel, Sammlung Online,
sammlungonline.kunstmuseumbasel.ch/eMuseumPlus.

Printed and bound in Great Britain by
Imprint Digital, Upton Pyne, Exeter

Marion Loffman
the kindest of wives

&

i.m. Harold Loffman (1919–1990)

Contents

I

Being, A Pear 15
On Dungeness Beach 16
C'mon Town! 18
Singularity at Boggle Hole 21
Beyond Top Withins 23
Companionship 25
Watercress in Kearsney 26
Classifying 'Together' 27
John Milton's Contention 29

II

Without Hull, at Night 33
A Dance That Will Not Die 35
Monument to the Red Soilers 37
Thomas Harriott's Discoveries 38
Overlooking the Calder 40
Visitation 42
The Second Flaming 43
The Singer 44
Night Lines 45

There Are Two St. Augustines, Matt 47

III

Concert in Yarmouk 57
Remembering Les 58
Bone Exile 60
Watch With Me 61
Scree at Pendle Hill 63
For You Have Been a Friend to Me 66
Winter Journey 67
Departure 68
No Longer on Our Screens 69

IV

Circling the Ash (1) 73
Along Great Gable 75
By Clear Water 77
From the Night Stall 78
Sketches of John Clare 80
Evening Pilgrimage 83
Cold and Shallow Waters 84
i.m. Mark Rothko 86
Circling the Ash (2) 87

Trying to Find Charles Olson's House 91

V

Future Haunting 107
Imagining Stonehouse 108
Endangered Species 112
The Thatched Barn 113
From the Quaker Graveyard in Idle 115
After All Hallows 118
Moor Haunts 119
Quell the Storm 120
A Still Passing 122

VI

Where Hart's Tongue Dwells 127
Kufaniya 128
Rebekahs at the Gate 129
Elpis, Daily 130
The Ornadels 131
Kath Comes Home 132
Musica Reservata 133
The Long Walk Home 135
Emerson's Tonic 136

Notes & Acknowledgements 139

Preface

I am indebted to Luigi Marchini, Jo Field, Trevor Breedon, Robert Marsh, Jen Kahawatte, Gary Michael Studley for their support. Thank you also to Fiona Sinclair (*Message In A Bottle*), Helen Ivory, and Kate Birch (*Ink, Sweat & Tears*), Nicholas Bielby (*Pennine Platform*) who have published some of these poems and to Nell Nelson and Cahal Dallat for their comments in workshop 'contexts' plus. Other poems have been published in *Sandwich Arts Week Anthology 2019*; *Canterbury Poet of the Year 2021*; and, *The Kentish Consortium Magazine* Autumn 2021.

Jamie McGarry's vision in establishing Valley Press has been a boon for many poets and readers of poetry. Peter Barnfather has been as helpful and insightful an editor as I could have wished for, my thanks to them both. Special appreciation to my dear cousin, David Loffman, for walking along this path with me. For our many exchanges, Pennine ventures and promptings a particular thanks to David Duffy.

I

Being, A Pear

Green and bruised by the core,
resting after feeling fresh to fading away
with the scent of an ending.
These peel remnants, mush supposedly,
a universe in themselves, flesh
fallen random from something timeless
and, after due process, sliced
or segmented, to fend for itself
without questioning or hiding away.

On Dungeness Beach

i.m. Alf Tart (1922–2016)

Sixty or seventy gulls standing still
meet in complete silence over me,
debris of rubber tubes, crab legs,
old net wires, grass specks by the road
beyond the shore, shacks to
shelter from the wind.
Why do they stand so still?
The rusted rail-tracks, lumber chewed
by insects, a makeshift path
for their feet to track to the sea.
The water sounds from right
to left, you can hear the tide
move across with your eyes closed,
with the wind sipping the sea.
Black wings, the gulls hunt parallel
to the surface of the sea, forays
every five minutes.

Still
sixty or seventy gulls, statues
over us as the water cover us.
A vigil for all the fisher-wives
who made fires at four in the morning,
lived in the cabins for years,
brought up sons and daughters,
buried in Lydd down the road,
or the men who worked the lifeboat
where you'd cling to rigging, to the dead.

Two hundred names saved in sixty
years – sixty gulls stand still; remember
the shrimping, or the lugworms,
hauling the nets by the side of the house
which would brush us wet-soaked,
wooden slats, cuffed by the wind's shout
on a beach with plastic bottles, butt-ends,
as water erodes my edges, as the sea
makes its motion inward and we are thrown
by a passing stranger into the water,
into the stone piles, into our past.

C'mon Town!

Power concedes nothing without demand.
It never did and never will.
– Frederick Douglass

Each day, hordes up Hunger Hill,
hope in replica kits, a new season
with yesterdays a filler that binds
we who shout, who stand together
with little wealth,
but worth
has a better measure.

Bunting and corncrake fly over,
and bluebells shift a fraction.
The trees that have survived
the building of service stations and motorways
bend by Elland as, far below,
a swarm of worker ants gnaw at wood
dressed in blue with white dashes.

We listen for the results – elections fixed,
spring hopes become iced winter,
ashes of the many pay bankers' holidays,
profits a distant conspiracy, a celebrity club
to leave us cold. A ground inspection,
the game will be on, its delayed for now
as cars fill roads, however many there are.

We praise players – Paterson, Norris,
the Flemings, Juryeff, and Super Geoff.
A brief sun nips the peaks,
and after graft we watch, march,
write messages on banners.
Coined anomic
under Leviathan's lash.

Wages in plastic sachets,
super-glued; to extract the small amounts
more than musings to the nine muses needed.
Hesperides' golden apples fell
along the grander estates.
Evening falls like a miner's hard hat hit by hard rock
as the moon skims the Calder and Hebble.

Small-time trophies are collected;
dates not forgotten in silver.
Young Dave Longhurst's tongue
swallowed near Bootham Bar,
the sluice-gates of tears, so near.
Under cloud cover. Under floodlights.
In all weathers.

Albert leathered goals and beer tasted better,
a slip and a slide slipping faster that passes by,
check performance levels by food banks,
as a curlew calls across the moor,
or snow covers and the wind blasts us
who walk by and are gone,
and the game goes on.

Icarus dreams, winks at the sun as glass
ceilings are kicked in, hopes are raffle tickets,
a lottery lost.
Austerity bites like crocodile teeth,
we see the croc smiles in hospitality boxes,
but here by the Skircoat
it's a bit different.

We pay the rising gate costs,
see balls kicked, tea brewed,
we could do with a win bonus besides cheering.
There is no trickle-down effect,
our nerve endings are raw,
Yorkshire! Shaymen! Bastard referee
whistles against us again.

Singularity at Boggle Hole

Beneath the vast sky it sits, the sea cyan
refracts back while white surf rushes above the blue.
My Baytown mug's ceramic mirrors
that same sea, that same sky.
Odd, if not singular, that its utility
is its empty space
whose parameter, so smooth to the lips,
is embedded. Such singularity
defies what is deified,
defines how much steaming tea
or coffee may be contained.
Thirst-quenching as that may be,
it resists, invisibly, telling the whole tale –

deep, into the spinning black forever,
this is the point.
A singularity to dwell upon. Far-flung,
versions of exoplanetary space spotted
while I look out over the North Sea
where post-Brexit fishing ground trawls
summon only light catches.
The dispossessed recall the bustle of high streets,
clamber around the built-up ceramics of life,
and, after labour, remain unheard,
left to ponder the singularity of existing
– isolated, exceptional, moveable
and removeable.

　　　　　　　　　　Now, so far apart
are Van Hove's densities from fish-filled nets.
You can watch it all from Boggle Hole,
the air salty, the barking of seals,
vapours over ripples of uncertainty,
of time and the incoming tide.
Contemplate what relevance this
or my mug's blue-and-white emptiness
has beneath
this vast unfolding sky.

Beyond Top Withins

*prompted by the Elmet of
Ted Hughes and Fay Godwin*

Fay focuses her lens to catch
two seated figures between sycamore sentries
whose branches crack as lightning blazes
briefly above them.

Wind shouts through Elmet's roofless relic
as they look beyond to moor and gritstone
where Emily's tale of broken bonds and shadows
compose a music heard in the horn of storms,

a curlew's stiffening cry before the chatter
of winter. Over bogland a heartfelt song,
moorland strong, cuts through frost,
drifts down Haworth's cobbled street.

December, up to the Parsonage. Brontë goods
cram shop-fronts. Emily's breath struggles
on the couch, beneath her forbidding glance,
no-one dares to challenge her. She is truly

liminal – by gravestone monuments
at darkness's edge, heralded by heather
and the far crags, framed in black-and-white.
This man and this woman

look to the outcrops that subsume them,
to the trees that shelter them,
under black-grey clouds that unfurl
while, above bilberry blight, light lances

stone-ragged walls that square
this ruin of the ages, the path that leads here
to the one hidden and trampled over
where all our ghosts await us.

Companionship

for Elaine Feinstein

A breeze blows fast and loose as we walk
arm-in-arm; your Cossack hat nods at me
under a metal grey September sky.

From the Pennines to the far Steppes
a bond, as intricate as any weaving,
ties us together; a meandering thread,
as of people in chains sewn into sackcloth
to be lost at gunpoint, their lines half-written.
Our backdrop, the *white light of the world*,
never darkens, refuses to fade.

We shuffle along, after laughter sit
together, surrounded by many windows
where words need not be spoken
and are never enough.

Watercress in Kearsney

Eider ducks float along the Dour
as a summer-kissed girl nets water-lilies.

Sun bursts between cumulus cloaks
and highlights the many-leafed canopy
found around mature trunks
where hideaway games jostle
with footballs and a day out
for the elderly, infirm and the family.

Gulls parade by the lake's edge,
where the weir-step of water curls,
carbonates. Kent flint-stone
is baking on the Kearsney walls.

Armed in our piquant flavouring,
we avoid liver fluke and Eristalis flies
that hover as we cluster;
green and white blossom
in a chalk water home,
and our hollow stems sway
in this ancient cressonnière.

Companionship

for Elaine Feinstein

A breeze blows fast and loose as we walk
arm-in-arm; your Cossack hat nods at me
under a metal grey September sky.

From the Pennines to the far Steppes
a bond, as intricate as any weaving,
ties us together; a meandering thread,
as of people in chains sewn into sackcloth
to be lost at gunpoint, their lines half-written.
Our backdrop, the *white light of the world*,
never darkens, refuses to fade.

We shuffle along, after laughter sit
together, surrounded by many windows
where words need not be spoken
and are never enough.

Watercress in Kearsney

Eider ducks float along the Dour
as a summer-kissed girl nets water-lilies.

Sun bursts between cumulus cloaks
and highlights the many-leafed canopy
found around mature trunks
where hideaway games jostle
with footballs and a day out
for the elderly, infirm and the family.

Gulls parade by the lake's edge,
where the weir-step of water curls,
carbonates. Kent flint-stone
is baking on the Kearsney walls.

Armed in our piquant flavouring,
we avoid liver fluke and Eristalis flies
that hover as we cluster;
green and white blossom
in a chalk water home,
and our hollow stems sway
in this ancient cressonnière.

Classifying 'Together'

It is a sorting beyond identity
or Role Models,
shelves are stacked, weighted
with a rich panoply of -ologies.
A library, knowledge
orchestrated
in alphanumeric code,
making a harmony of neighbours
like a consort of shawms and rebecs,
crumhorns in company,
snakes and nakers
with sackbuts to round off, all
augmenting a choir who lift this broken consort
into a *unity of varieties* that reaches out
to scale heights as if in celebration,
like a winter summiting of K2
traversed, despite the Abruzzi Ridge,
rock-falls, ice-breaks and oxygen lacks,
when no incident blights the descent.
A system where Religion and Technology
are ordered without tension, labelled
sparingly on book-spines housed,
if fading, in digital time.
All authored while dismissing prejudice,
a rich collection delighting
in every moment an alphabet of being brings.
I wait to be issued with the songs
and sonatas, to permit
an intricate arrangement where Peace
is not a distributed relative.

Dated wall-signs that declaim
Education and History as far apart,
demean what Brit or compassion might be,
are binned. Is that all there is? you ask.
Pollution like Planets is not so distant
but Dewey's logic places finger-holds
for scaling heights
in linear progression – *if only* –
or counterpoint as a single voice or line.
There is the august Ranganathan,
where every theme has a place
where each instrument has time to be heard,
as a lute-strum conjures a galliard
for us to dance without division,
as inclusive as love, when night,
the intimate dark, comes sublime
blended together,
until the sun stops.

John Milton's Contention

If the day is defined by virtue
or some ethical growth
like the dancing blue of forget-me-nots
which spread generously
even upon an unpromising path,
apply with care, see how
they range freely without evasion,
face the wind full-on as it spreads
seeds from the many pistils
to germinate random places,
to reveal a display to warm another
as the sun warms the soil.

Contrarily, in a darkening night
if this virtue is both cloistered and fugitive,
unexercised so not to confront difficulty,
unbreathed, a ghost to haunt intentions,
silhouette the hesitant who emerge
from cloisters in shadow, to avoid
conscience, hidden in heat and dust
unlike the forget-me-nots that,
however the wind blows,
dance in their growth of perfect blue,
swing in syncopated time,
neither fugitive nor cloistered.

II

Without Hull, at Night

Night-walking,
round Terry Street, Auckland Avenue,
all you do at 62, hidden behind closed curtains,
all I want behind the closed doors.
A car cuts a corner
headlights   images   shapes
a verge by shops, empty spaces inside, vacant
except the impossibility of sleep.
You won't meet me by the Land of Green Ginger
on Avs of honeysuckle like Marlborough with
Arnetts dawn-fresh bakes in Spring Bank,
far from the food bank.
A shelf of offers
makes a difference for others –
the hand moves on the clocktower,
all things will pass.

Night-scarring,
alone and elderly, she stumbles,
a ground floor silhouette
revealed by lamplight.
Her inner voice wrestles
the sinew of being awake
with the hardship of being wakeful
in her bedroom, darkly.
You won't meet me by the docklands –
pride languishes by wharf and Stoneferry,
the factory shifts gone
where welding once was.

Pints to cool the feel of furnace heat
to cope with night's North Sea tides
in a home as close as Hessle,
as near as Brough.

Night-howling,
the fox and I scavenge street bins
before collections come
dazed by daylight.
Maybe it's a Tuesday,
insomnia confuses. The pain
to awake one day to see you
with some stranger
at daybreak.

A Dance That Will Not Die

for the lost Adderbury Village Morris Team

What's in that field? Some scarecrow gone to grass,
bright blades tall as wheat before the harvest,
a glorious summer day, a steel sparkle in the eye,
raise a glass, chime out loud, beware Mischief coming
for come he does in many guises. Can you see?

What's the pub's sign? A hobbyhorse and caper,
days before combine harvesters and factory farms,
where a twist of barley in your lapel shows
you're ready to work well, do more than the Hey!
The hired line step forward on command. Who's there?

Who's beneath the clock-tower? Shin-bells sound,
clap the willow sticks, mayhem in double-step time,
the hour strikes, crowds assemble for the spectacle,
it's the Day of the May, gather on this common ground,
whizz-bang! Was that a photo flash?

What's outside the hall? Engines but no cars,
no ring-tone to be heard, and doors bolted.
Some metal shards on a path where weeds multiply,
a fence just cut wire, are those wild poppies
bending red against the breeze?

Now a team dances by the Smithy's house.
Charley survived, the rest knocked out the way.
Never again the rattle and bells, bullets and shells
replaced the beer and banter of pre-War days,
each ghost he can see, dancing Blunt's steps.

What now? Don top hats, baldricks and Fool's mask,
tune the fiddle, stretch the bellows, chorus loud,
The Buffoon will hit you hard – one step out of line
and more than a pig's bladder will belt you,
no health and safety will save you,

but we won't forget,
and we won't stop the dance.

Monument to the Red Soilers

Fires scorch eight hundred feet drops,
neither rag nor chain pumps
divert or block gushing waters,
just pick your way through hazard tunnels
which dim candles briefly lit.

Other side of the rocks, faint knocks.
Flame and flood, a race and conflict over lead
as Red Soilers and Magpie Maypits race.
Three Red Soilers were smoke-stuffed –
no company name change dries widows' tears.

I walk in stone-walled uplands near Sheldon
by the 'smithy. The shafts remain
darkly silhouetted against the sky.
Along the winding Wye, limestone outcrops,
this *perfect relic*. We wander beyond

distant Assizes, the choking cries fade
as memories barely hear Victorian curses
or smell the overcoming smoke.
An industrial treasure, the taken breath
to those who delved, and dug deep.

Thomas Harriott's Discoveries

Chasing fundamentals has strange dangers;
science as heresy, tears for Erasmus. Unpublished,
Thomas saw light waves obliquely
mirror new angles, knew an atomism where
minute particulars transform base metal
to dream-wealth. Experimental,
but who will recall?

Come closer – pack lives into trunks that feature
cartographic asides, the precise lines explore
the Americas as far as Roanoke.
Sick over the Atlantic, you shared a vision
as far as the moon's seas, not mere optics
lenses to unknown trajectories,
come closer.

Back from the Atlantic, you piled
cannon balls like spheres for the ages
from conjecture to Virginia,
up and down, waves and capstans.
The high stakes, Bruno aflame,
the scattering of ashes,
such civilisation.

Time to invent logarithms, interest accruing,
or create Algonquin fo-net-ics
with Wanchese and Mateo. Meanwhile,
sunspots telescoped reveal heavens anew.
A biography shaded like a lunar valley,
a history unheralded,
an unveiling.

Overlooking the Calder

Hell Hole Rocks overlook
my early rise up Cuckoo Steps
to Heptonstall Old Church.

Wind bites from Stoodley Pike
while, ready to unfurl flood waves,
the Calder murmurs at sand bags.

On weathered gravestones,
PG, SG and MG are carved
beneath roofless arches.

Behind windows and gritstone walls
a figure appears, a brief scent
of lilac passes and is gone.

Her mischief was a balm,
a light play of finger-tips on the back.
A Syrinx memory conjures shadows.

Strangers, ignorant of such hauntings,
pass over these cobbled centuries
by bilberry and crowberry.

Water swirls spectral by the weir,
a rabbit scurries by, ready
like me, to risk the hill-top

to hear the clatter of tractors
where the skeletons sink
above sloping terraces.

I yaw against the wind.

Visitation

They open the door.
They walk by.

I am a frieze, a statue
frozen in black feathers
on a bureau in white shite fear
peppered upon printed papers.
Even Achalanatha's head has turned,
not me, no muscle moves.

A dive, a chimney hole
was unexpected, my muffled cry
unheard. No way
to claw back
musty darkness.

Five nailed snakes creep closer,
I leap away to the nearby stool,
spot the open door
hop quick   skip out.

To return home,
a murmuration
high around gables, I stretch
safe, shake off the smell of it.
How the trembling ends.

The Second Flaming

Longer than Grindleford tunnel,
a musky damp of not being lived-in,
the sort of dank where all is lost and gone,
folk shake under ganister in fear,
trapped, each thought hacked.

The labour brought and bonded here,
it's okay to stare or look away, choices are difficult.
How was the brick top curved
under limestone, sandstone and grit?
Down the walls ancient sweat drips.

Arson orange flames at one end,
each flare exposes faces of the fallen,
who mouth their pain, their screams,
from *chacun pour soi* their squalls
pierce each course and stretcher in these walls.

But there is a second flame
slow burning behind the shadows.
It starts to kindle and to blaze
an incandescence in the dark,
to redeem the struggle of their days.

The Singer

In your arms I fly
skywards, a lark
charmed towards a blue heaven
as the sun spotlights
your eyes, your mien, your sound.

Where your voice sings,
pleasures entice both eye and ear.
You smile complete as you catch
your breath. Your lips open, thrill
as your arpeggio ascends.

Sweet summer air intoxicates
my senses in rose perfume:
aquamarine and ever green
gladden. Foxgloves
sway in the wind's shuffle.

As an oboe's note, I soar
winging into a promise
where *all things are made good.*
A theorbo strums; the melody,
like a silver dress, shimmers.

Night Lines

Disedged or curbed,
deconstruct the dark and light,
we pass transient as showers,
step gingerly to miss pavement cracks
while rain rods and chrome gleams
accelerate through amber
in case the lights change,
in case someone dares to use
token crossings. Either way,
we are dwarfed below
neon white. A night scene seeps
into consciousness
where towers overhang,
rocket skyward
and we, mere chromosome collections,
adrift in this infinite,
shuffle and shadow while trading profits
invest in Ashlon and hurricane glass,
covers, with a brutal front, a space
to match a commerce to flaunt
some well-appointed selves.
But we, unnoticed behind windows
or blanked out in black,
head for home
like charged and random particles,
question being, cossetted
in Calpol or cocaine,
lost beyond ever wider roads,
blunted, but edgy.

There Are Two St. Augustines, Matt

Why enter unwelcome lands
               when only a prior,
with forty frocked pilgrims,
               brave the weather
for winds and arrows
               make sharp incursions?
Are Canterbury and Hippo so far apart?

After all,
what's a common name
               commonly held?
Consider an essay
        time-bound
with modern deadlines.
It demands completion,
             an answer,
                 a result.
Do we look to today
or have eyes for tomorrow?

Souk Ahras so unfashionable,
Souk Ahras so unknown,
Souk Ahras barely on a map,
difficult to find
even on the train from London Victoria, Matt;

even for the exalted high
                who forsake
                              such backwaters.
Does using instant messaging
                make us so different?

Homilies, confessions and the unhappy soul appear
in different places
        to each generation
                 never mind the dates.

Ambitions
      fostered by families
           (or their absence),
distant fathers,
        mysteries
and the geography of fear

arranged in Papal orders,
                          sacrament and vestiges
of old gospel tales,
    resurrections,
        day-to-day sacrifices,

as if a student loan would cover this,
Studies Save Lives
        for eternity,
               creed
        but challenge now,
this is what eternal life depended upon.

      Do we have such verities
or certainties
      in this land of fame-seeking,
            of fortune hunters
where Warhol's fifteen minutes
            exaggerates the truth?

You travelled to Canterbury
            dear son
in hopes to finding –
      he travelled
from safety with St. Anthony, quickly
thought better of staying around Thanet.
            Gregory made sure
he thought better of his thought.

      What impelled your travel –
            a getting close to a beginning?
A protreptic of Cicero, Hortensius?
            Might Ambrose inspire?

Lost in research papers, theories and prone to critique,
academics wash their hands,
consider their next fence,
as governments lay targets at their well-considered doors.

Souk Ahras not many doors,
Souk Ahras not many fences,
exaltations open to myriad stars,
the vast universe of skies,
the Pleiedes and Orion
light the hopes and passions of another.

    Also
Augustus wondered
    at shimmers on coastal settings,
strange chords
    never heard in Ethelbert's England,
a music of deserts, heat and wholeheartedness
    to add Wisdom to the ages,
        an awakening dawn.

Adeodatus,
    Adeodatus;
a dance that makes a better day.
Adeodatus,
    Adeodatus,
breathe in me,
    prayers of long searching,
acts of hope and contrition;
recall anniversaries,
essay deadlines,
    last minute flurries,
inelegant and clumsy style –
can you make a degree or religion
        out of such coarse materials?

Gregory thought so to force his namesake
    to Canterbury
with its deadly traffic system,
               long recoveries from blitz and bombs
whose Gregorian chants
        incant
              a long way from Souk Ahras.
African Latin,
a beat and pain stabs deep,
even for a bishop –
    Adeodatus,
           Adeodatus
– times together are so precious.

He loved in Carthage, Milan;
how do you grade places to learn:
Oxford, Heidelberg? By results?

A decade of secret loving,
            intense embraces and still
one mark short of a First!

So,
    from Gregory's mandates
        founding posh schools
    to dedicate to the feasts of martyrs

            born two weeks distant
   – Tagaste to Hammersmith a few miles apart;

  the nurse
    closed curtains
      as the light speared in
        as you cried out to welcome this life,
I knew as little as Hippo
    to help give you a good life,
        start your journey strong,
to bring some centre,
    a sense of being, of flaming lights
beyond grades,
Halifax defeats and brass,
       a clear day.

'You flashed,
    shone,
      …dispelled my blindness.'

'Recall prayer
for the in-dwelling spirit,
remembering
God has no need of your money,
      but the poor have.'

We don't need to gather
      vestments and relics, felicities,
favours from the great and the good;
     they will come
        and go

without our help
>	– perhaps in the end,
Pelagius, Donatism,
is more powerful
>	than Vatican centres,
>	>	Bulls and Popemobiles.
That our own virtue
>	may earn us credit,
>	>	merit despite all.
Perhaps
>	amidst beer cans,
>	>	good company, daily pressure points,
we might enter this –
>	a new felicity,
>	>	life full
>	>	and worth living.

III

Concert in Yarmouk

for Aeham Ahmad

From street cries in a Spring Damascus
to bomb blasts and the leaving of Yarmouk.
An acidic theme rains on lives
and their endings.
Despite the rubble, the ruins of homes,
a pianist plays in the street, surrounded
by children singing in unison.
A minor key amidst the ravages of war.

Zaineb sang for relief. Snipered,
she bleeds lifeless by the music shop
where instruments await players
who have abandoned Yarmouk.
Another explosion shatters more homes,
the shop stays untouched.
The owner's hands cover his face,
he cannot play another chord.

So many keys lost after the planes pass,
all outcome is veiled as sea-mist.
This sound memory is a life jacket
bobbing on an empty sea.
Zaineb, the chorus and piano become
scattered jetsam on a tidal wave
of steel. Silence remains,
and a stilled heart.

Remembering Les

A punch in the face that never happened,
a cup of tea, arm-wrestling sons,
winning; around a bollard by the Blue Bell
you wrapped a car. At the top of Carr Lane
we waited for news. A marine,
from three-mile walks at 78 daily,
to a room with a view and a tumour.
Lending us the Viva to Black Sail Pass,
we drank whisky, laughed,
shared stabs of love lost.
Years of Shipley night shifts' furnace fire,
then asleep on the settee.
Go for it, you told me in the hospice
where we smuggled vodka to gulp and forget
the well-manicured garden, this last bedroom.
You said, *See you at Christmas*.

You steered your own course.
At the wedding the Watersons part-singing,
The worst bleeding music I've ever heard –
we laughed and played some more!
You gave up forty Woodies a day
grandson Ben didn't want you to die.
We stumbled down Thackley Road after
Jack's funeral, Ice-Box in the distance,
traffic shot past quicker than the years;
Wrose beyond Idle, houses on the hill
like ancient ramparts. If you step on
his rose, carefully grown out the front,
just see what he'll do – no coughs,
but in October they drew the curtains.
A kettle boils. *Have a cup, Jeff lad*,
I hear from the next room.

Bone Exile

The worst day. Love becomes ugly,
rain hits horizontal in the eyes,
drains mumble and spit in the silence,
through frosted windows the wind chills
as trees bend on my obscure road,
roof slates crack and fall
and all shrinks to nothing.

There is a surreal feel to this fall,
like a sudden acceleration down Losehill
or like a fox flattened on the road,
all blooded bone and matted fur,
no hint of heaven or after-life.
What life within is left?

This numb ache of not belonging
while grey cumulus clouds surrounds, empty
like a clown whose laughter is lost,
whose make-up drips, whose flesh leaks
alongside. I am reduced to this bone
no longer home.

Watch With Me

i.m. Cicely Saunders (1918–2005)

Its what you leave behind,
the quiet intense look of it
as breath slowly regains,
                for the moment,
its rhythm.
It's the domestics – money, clothes, photos,
a child's anguish. Rest
is being tucked-in at night,
an ear to hear these words,
                      the last
while wind-gusts sound on the shore
as this ripple of living
comes to a close.

Pain is managed,
the slow injecting of relief.
To move and yet be moved,
to console yet be consoled.
                      Treasure is
this moment
for the value of time, like the seas,
is a matter of depth.

No mere moment then
but a lifetime in a nod or
in your eye that watches,
as you hear this coda
while the voice's familiar tone
slowly fades

         as grief,
like a coble bobbing on the tide,
passes by.

Scree at Pendle Hill

I

Metal pins heal warts, ground-to-cloud lightning
strikes the summit, nightmares the yellow sun
of St. John's Wort might soothe,
arthritic relief in turmeric. To not conform

threatens elites, *Witch! Witch!*
Chattox and Demdyke cauldrons stirred,
blind daemons lit, clay figures fired;
after a feud the hanging, a short drop.

Mix ginger, a dash of rosemary, catnip
and calendula for ease, cinnamon to tame the bloods.
Hygiea comes in different forms, so relief

for the Pendle sick, clouds thicken
like a ravens' unkindness. This barometer
sees dense air, pressure and mercury soar.

II

More recent steeples rule the landscape of our lives,
monthly salary slips a rent for our souls,
digitised tithes from our poor scratchings
of labour around these lands.

Some say this is years ago, of course, when scars were fewer,
when I could climb Pendle quicker,
and change was a Word away.

III

Lancashire downpours; we walk among moorland trees
clothes sodden. It dampens the ardour for the climb.
Black rain has darkened mid-days here,
and you say, *Walk on.*

I breathe in, aim for the ascent
with the roofs and chimneys in sight below.
With each stride I lean on my walking stick,
you sprint up. Relentlessly.

A John Law curse still drips even as we reach the height.
We ignore the omens and dark whispers and fake cures
from this wild hall of history,

I seize hand-sized pieces of scree at my feet
and spell, without thought,
Be valiant for the truth.

For You Have Been a Friend to Me

for Jack and Carol

The pendulum swings, the clock clucks,
between each swing a vista, on the face of it,
from Windhill to a Bridlington fancy.
Can the Unmoved Mover be revealed?
Such things go in circles – in circles we raced
looking for Jason, lost in the woods,
then led with words as through a dense forest,
able to make do, we watched as the kids grew.
Older now, we're ready to rest, watch a toddler,
no Valerio, approach uncertainly –
a grandchild with a grin, red-faced, breathless;
these moments remain undiminished.
While I stare at the urn on the mantle, Clio
boils the kettle, scribbles on a scroll, summarises
our lives' trochleae which only we can recall,
tears fall, and the pendulum swings
as the chapel's curtains close like iron grids.

Winter Journey

i.m. Johann & Caspar David Friedrich

I have thrown crutches away
on frozen snow where fir tree steeples
silhouette distant shadows. My back leans
on a pew of rock, raises my eyes on high.
I wear my dead brother on my back, hidden
under ice-lake cracks seeking solace –
a room to warm the oncoming night,
a prayer to lighten the weight, to gently
close the door on a December memory,
to tidy away the surrounding mist.

The path is a *sea of ice*,
I cannot walk beyond these firs,
I try to sing *The Good Old Way*
but you cannot hear. You only catch
a profile, a deep grey sky,
here by a darkening boulder,
a resting place.
As snow falls lighten,
you may follow me, brother,
like wind into the vast distance
beyond the snow-line.

Departure

A palm held out, fingers stretch,
time to linger, as if to leave
will be a loss. Still so much to see,
we part too hurriedly,
we grieve whatever we believe.

Flags are folded, best books bundled,
a generation's photos are packed.
We map the labyrinths of our past
that our words and deeds may last.
Memories like furniture will be stacked.

Our blurred eyes try to meet, but we know
what all this signifies:
its time to go, time to go.

No Longer on Our Screens

Here, in the middle, Abu Aqleh,
from Ramallah protests to Shabak's snipers.
After the rifle's crack, you are scattered
across the West Bank, a burning
inflamed or forgotten, a Gaza motif
to the sound of rocket strikes
launched here, landing there.

I picture you on camera,
brown-eyes in frowned questioning,
dressed in crimson, a golden dome behind,
filmed above the roof-tops with PRESS
on your flak jacket for all to witness
by the wailing, along the Wall, clear
as a bullseye in any target range.

You are still the unheard voices,
the muzzled many, in the rubble of daily life,
who bleed or live to go beyond camps
beyond Nakbah to a day,
one day, to sing by the waters,
secure by the sea, along the Jordan.
Shireen. Al Jazeera. Good Night.

IV

Circling the Ash (1)

Unnerving
with Sirius and Epsilon Eridani so close,
I orbit this ash tree of shining loam
round this well-worn track
as if in another life.

Like me, Eridani b has arrived
marginally. Odd to settle here
where there is doubt, no hills
and, between each branch,
this star-spotted panoply dotted

like memories that are not mine,
but feel as they should be,
like a shadow or suspended sentence.
Some write of loss. Some are lost.
Some brood upon a better place.

I hear distant voices, rumour
buzzing like tinnitus in my ear.
I look around, consider dieback,
wings flap, arms brush past,
some sacred water burns at the roots.

Howls in grey, other cries strike crimson.
I follow my footprints round the trunk,
like a satellite on a pre-ordained path,
always a hum of distant fugues, of timeless
fires. A long, wordless night.

I tremble, entangled in fine-teeth leaflets
bunched beneath the twisting branches,
so many ways and count-downs to here.
Compelled, I circle the trunk again.
To commemorate, to somehow

communicate with a presence,
to recall some lost or past life
this sculpted trunk contains;
a face before me, spreads like lesions,
insisting order is here, that all will be well

despite a deepening dark and wild edges.
If so, this strange insistence
chills.
Why should it
not be?

Along Great Gable

The path up and down is one and the same…
– Heraclitus

Arrived above Little Hell Gate
which, briefly,
had been beside us. Standing up,
wind smacked,
rain spat but
clear by Westmorland's cairn
round Stone Cove
up Moses Trod path.

The high trill of wood warbler
is heard as we survey the path
where also, winging silently,
glides the goshawk on the hunt.

It's been years
since that first ascent
when we learnt to secure footholds,
drank from the full glass,
swore to view horizons
beneath Gable Crag's boulder
by Grey Knotts,
then aim for Wasdale.

Can there ever be enough vistas
or stone-packed paths
for mud-caked boots,
ageing and stained green,
still to tread?

The descent speeds us
beyond knee strains or struggles
to our arrival
this very moment.

By Clear Water

Even without Hubble, I see
galaxies in front of me, yet no thing behind.
Each leaf and flower is here
yet this seeing is a pause in a process.
In the mirror my face is transformed
into those who have gone before,
and will go after, the wind from each breath,
the horizons found in every eye.

Cherry blossom showers,
ash, oak and silver birch
rising to the sun, as if awakened.
Here is my dwelling, this clearing in the wood,
this valley hidden beneath the peaks
where clear water flows ice-blue, rushing
to remind me of the miracle of home.

From the Night Stall

Shawl over my head, lit by the stall's light,
I am roasting chestnuts dwarfed beside pagodas
that locked doors hours ago. A stranger wearing,
oddly, a flat grey cap appears taller and glides
cloaked archaically in a green frock coat.
He stares wide-eyed from across the riverside.
Perhaps, along with the branch-hung lanterns
walking by the Canal for the first time,
he is surprised to see my stall open and me,
chatting with my friend, so late.

The only sounds are scooters that motor along
where this figure stands impervious,
as silent as the dark. A thousand lights dance
alongside the Hangzhou Canal. Opposite,
Celebration Hall overlooks us all.
No-one to buy roasting nuts,
occasional couples pass by like the tide,
a lone youth sits attached to a smartphone,
eager to connect and press keys.

The ten-storey yellow-lit tower
blinks red as if to celebrate
from the summit. What
can the stranger see?
He seems masked, a silhouette,
not even a *Nihao* is spoken.
I look but he has vanished.
I warm my hands over the embers,
wonder at passing strangers
on this still Huai'an night.

Sketches of John Clare

for Anna

I

Some scran in a cool breeze
by Emmonsail Heath,
a *distance from the town*;
but home was a quiet mind
before the two elms died.

You are a winging in the clear air,
supping the sheer wonder of words,
little trotty wagtails, the widest of skies,
not just scrawled poems
on paper scraps.

Kop kop carthorse loaded with dreams,
desires, stacked images, assiduous
this ambition for life, for *starnels whizz*
and *grey beard jackdaws noise*
a backdrop near.

Not just *in the suds*,
by a nightingale's nest,
hear *a wooden cuckoo sing* –
but then to sleep alone, cold
in the hedgerows.

O there is your green meadow,
your *crooking brooks*
to carefully catch these traces
piled on a cart, the straight road
out of Helpston.

II

John becomes Randall the bloodied boxer,
arms up high, pumped in triumph,
each memory particle deftly removed.
Despite protests, enclosures surround you,
your likeness now but a death-mask.

Now a lord, Byronic phrases rhyme
next to straw plaiting time, stone picking
stains your smock. Night's candle
could reveal Patsy, the wife
of another life, too many miles away.

Visited by a *sneering clown*,
some moneyed strangers blind
to your wealth, reveal their poverty.
Yesterday's faded fashion, media memory
replaces you for another find.

III

Through Thunderidge and Roydon
along with Tom Porter,
your *confidential* Sunday friend,
spot with delight stitchwort,
birds' nests and common mallow.

Scrape your fiddle, dance,
cavort while your beer spills,
a merry round between caravans,
and Mary, full-hearted,
        always beloved.

Evening Pilgrimage

We meander between the sacred and secular.
Topography prompts response
where farms and barns on hills roll away
as I look north, beyond dry-stone walls.
An ochre ray of sun descends
upon this journey to a church
whose steeple aims towards heaven,
with its testament and history.
We see its quoins and square tower;
it squats, a distant silhouette.
We tread a sometime-travelled path,
wild and ill-defined, that casts doubt
on whether our *tom-tom* is accurate.
Sundown turns golden beneath the tree-line.
We venture on, haunted by figures
behind yew shapes, whose shadows make
icons which lodge at journey's end.
A bass-note organ resonates,
swirls as a whirlpool of air
winding around sycamore trunks.
We clamber over stiles. Disturbed
signs point ambivalently.
We hear hymns and high voices while
the sky glows red over the far hills.
The day has worn its twilight clothes.
Bells toll the sound of sermons,
Jeremiah's warnings, the tests of Job.

Our feet are sore, our knees worn through,
the benches too hard for comfort
but our eyes are lifted
to the gargoyles who warn against
our discrete erosions.

Cold and Shallow Waters

The beach, pebbles and sharp edges,
sea-spray reduces sight.
The Street all sand and stone,
they walk along in silence.
A wave at ankle height
laps along, foams around, stops
in shallow waters. Cold wind blows
the shallow waters, such cold waters.

Every afternoon in Tankerton
a child dies, every afternoon.
Two figures circle the beach huts
and the day is a lost, sobbing toddler.
Storm clouds billow and the storm cracks,
no gull's song whistles in the wind
when I found you amongst the groynes
near shallow waters, such cold waters.

A body lies beached by the sailing club
where clothes and eyes are sodden.
Archangel of cold, ice winds
stab your face and an exposed neck,
shake like sea campion blown, shivers
bindweed, mourning on the Slopes.
A telephone call, distant cries,
Was it quick? Who died?
By the shallow waters, such cold waters.

i.m. Mark Rothko

I want to stop the blood
gushing from your veins,
red rectangles, clear mirrors,
yellow distances, blue water
blocks. By the Sher-mah,
beyond the Four Seasons
the centre draws you – gallery,
home, or monastery –
wall-length quadrilaterals
red-and-black, on the right,
left, onward, outward, in-
ward – so many pass by,
then, entranced into, by and
for the colours that form,
melts into radiance, transfixed,
some eyes rest as if
touching a greater Self;
uncomprehending,
a man in a suit steps past quicker,
a mother drags her toddler
as if she was screaming,
Get me out of this.
Meanwhile, far beyond
Houston Chapel, no
decoration, more a journey,
sometimes it is good to grieve,
necessary to weep;
a triptych of horizons, hopes,
and tears.

Circling the Ash (2)

Strange
how brewing winds ignore borders,
how dark breeds imagined images,
how all-pervading power is time-bound,
chalara fraxinea.
The trunk carved into ten thousand facets,
from each branch a flag-face hangs
whose bat-shapes squeal
a Babel tower cacophony
that drives me on as I orbit
this dysfunctional immune system
under an uncanny ceiling of stars.
A shadow figure is suspended above
with a face so contorted
mouthing some redundant belief
untranslatable,
whose time has passed,
like a hulk turned senile
warning of what is
or will be.
Branches enfold this sight,
a web-like collection of veins throb
with green blood pulsing.
The roots gnarled, the sky darkens,
a mix like some cosmic compound.
Lesions spread and with each cry out
from the trunk the many fungal faces
who stare impoverished while, as I look
back, the figure hangs helpless.

What frees each branch from flags,
what renders these cries translatable
when the tree's crown is shattered,
its bark compacted?
Some wonder pathogens perhaps,
defensins that do not distort
vision, a myth for today.
Surely, the disease insists
a cure,
some meaning
may be found.

Trying to Find Charles Olson's House

I

But where is it? In the space between
ink and vellum, the end of the line.
Black Mountain myth Black Mountain Maximus
where the letter, stress and syllable on the page   these
       were my thoughts as I prepared for sleep.

               Dreams happen unawares.
I snuggled into duvets   a sentimental journey, the old days,

as if
     poetry mattered, not horror headlines in Kampuchea's
Killing Fields or Kenyan Kenyatta's Mau Mau risings.
You taught
from the book from the word from the page from the line,

you were where the future was to become

   real, but
in a better way, no confessional indulgences
not an easy journey then,
                 across
           the sea, the restless sea –
no turning back

                      to discover the making of a nest,
the clearing that enables the building of home,
the breath giving oxygen to the page,
    this was the house sought,
wasn't it? I thought.

                     Athene and adverbs go together
much like making large and being big, doing
is not merely recording but, beyond the senses, a stamp
non-erasable on the flatbeds of my daily exertions.

   Is this war, is this wisdom? Some say that this
is the human condition,
       reality
                as witnessed on screens
    in living rooms, its enough to watch and wait, not do.
Death comes without having to sprint towards it,
by a sharp blow of wisdom-sword perhaps,
Athene?

Whatever,   I was looking for his house,
came upon Hymie, the second-hand furniture dealer
with a place on a dream-street between Hull and horizons,
speaking to the young man I was,
not the bald and grizzled shape I became,
                it was not always like this;
                            mirrors reveal.
I was looking for the house and Hymie
      was selling me some furniture old-style,
about to be my landlord.

My friend advised, its good to have locks and keys,
its been a long time since we resided here, sensible
to change.
I left him to secure the accommodation, with Hymie talking.

The rest is a blur, like fog in the dewy morning,
or what happened
on your tenth birthday when Aunt Sophie
drank rather more than
expected.

        Perhaps   the singular space   optimally
is present, the very now and matter of things
red wheelbarrows even.

We are poured out like water,
confessed a man called Cal
    slumped with sonnets in an armchair, considering
    his lost ancestors.
    I strolled on, until
        suddenly
            I am planted
on an avenue of terraced dwellings fit for students.
I open a gate, walk four paces, to a small step by the door
push the bell,
from the upstairs window,
thickly German-accented, a woman with grey and honey hair,
spectacles, shouts,

He's further along,
                I'm glad you know, I
didn't expect that,
she would take me, lead me, guide me, she knew
he was a BIG man, *Oversized*, she chuckled.
Of course she knew him –
he would stride along the road regularly,
muttering about Athene and wisdom and the sword of
                breath and line.

                It was not a straight road.

      Nor was it paved with material possessions
or retail outlets, fashion vistas, or the fly-by-nights.
You could see this
        straight away!
        Curtains, veils and blinds in so many windows
        both French and Bay,

How was it built? I ask, naively.
With due form and frozen music, after all, a college
                is a community for learning,
and the building straight out of Emerson inferences, reflects
the shape and variety of trees, the entanglement of wonder
which are branches *bending the bow* and the *form of women*.
With this debate I moved down the street, no-
            one could notice any difference.

Was anyone there? Were the streets empty?
I was only aware of her humming
these songs of frozen music, Corbusier and glass
the promise of mountains,
He wasn't just BIG, he was a Mountain,

        they all

            up
         looked
              to him.

There was a time when professors of today
were enthusiastic and young, would
  rejoice in the space –

    Ahab, peg-legged, stood in front of me
    Shocked, I tried to hold his eyes, frozen
    At me, as if recruiting me, as if needing
    Someone unafraid of being incorrect, would
    Prepare the harpoon, patiently watch,
    Empathise with the need to complete a job
    Half-done; *There are no waves here Ishmael,*
    Gone the docks and boats and
    Flotsam of my tale, only the essence remains,
    These fragments hold back the current
    For fashion may flood the verities of seeing
    And being, and we each must find our Moby.

Maybe,

>   but deconstruct Stoic fire and Derrida and differences
>   are marginal; the singularity of time and space
>   make it all rather small, as small as a chromosome,
>   an atlas of being

in a breath, in a line, sing it sound it play it,
it is a chorus and reprise, how alike we are.
Would a woodpecker spot any differences amongst us, or care?

I have befriended the outriders, the subversives,
the hunters and poachers,
I have sought their honour code amidst the cloud cover
of their daily trudges across cities and savannahs,
across ages and Dante's ninth circle.
Still amongst strangers
and I am at a loss
and I am at –

II

the danger of betrayals   of mistrust   of mistake or mishap,
we are, after all,
but human

here,
    at last.

Take off your shoes.
In the street's centre? With traffic about to come?
This is not prophecy, I hear the engines thrum,
as an experienced pedestrian, well-versed in the highway code
I could see sense and no sense.
    She screeched, *Take off your shoes, walk barefoot.*
Film videotone and strange sorcery must be here.
                               This was
                   a road fit for studies.

The angle of starlight   sunlight
the yellow-horned poppy whose seed-pods
explode and spread as we pass, the sparrow-
seed gathering from a bird table between thorns and thistles
like an ark resting on Mount Judi,
impressive jay striking blue balanced on the front fence
        nuts in his beak, pondering to fly or to retrieve
a nightingale under the canopy of sycamore and ash while

over there,

crowds huddle by the bargain furniture shop
with its neat benching and
coffee tables.

I wandered;   bluebells
              hazed in their crowd,
              dazed as if seeing this
              the first time,
              background bass and drum reverberates
the clink of bottles, parties, hormones wild
with youth and passion and
cheap wine, no pinot noir near, a search for the grand cru
and still I have to stride. *Come, come*, she says again.
She rasps words in staccato.

    Mojos over
        hedgerows,
            IMPORT GREY SQUIRRELS,
                EXPORT LIVE SHEEP.

Trucks full pass by as thoughts, a motorway of emotions,
forever overtaking and the dreaded middle lane slowcoach
– you know the one – him with bare feet following
    this Levertov – eyes at the back of her head –
    shepherding him beyond *vers libre*.

Be, Be, Be! she rasps endlessly
      amidst iced minims of her whistles
sharp breves all on a note, acoustic echo like Gregorian chant,
quavers pierce scales, and the bass drum hum snored at
by old boilers and the central heating
of the experiences of the elders
who've seen it but never quite did it,
      not hemlock for Socrates,
      some herbal fusion would have been better.

Spot an estampie fused in the corner,
wired to the spot, consider the deficit of fact or how
      interpretations vary based on
sets of data, it's all crunched up like MS-DOS
            and as forgotten,
              the left-over is nothing changes
yet all has changed.

      Still
          barefoot
                in the dark
but she has been lost,
this angel of the avenues, who somehow spotted you from afar
with such harsh love – helps me on my way even before
the road block, traffic lights scarlet shone
                and the shadows danced
        in flame's flicker from a nearby garden
voices, even a chorus, a reprise and the smell

   of both savoury and sweet, cuisine of flavourings,
succulent, whisp-like on the breeze, tasting
   before I realise – sandals had somehow been put on!

I awoke to these stirrings –
   felt I was near.   Almost there.

  image metaphor reflection

   snow flakes the garden –
   what is seen from high windows,
   snowballs and laughter.

I consult the map and guideposts; over-engineered
so many icons to choose,
as if, in number,
truth accuracy legitimacy must be somehow
held.
  I stare at my hands, consult contours,
spot the landmarks – steeple, postbox and palace,
at least sandals keep my feet from the cold…

but I, who have never been to the States,
   must conjure fields as if the circles of hell,
   the promise of paradise were reference points,
   a cultural heritage but
         something to do with
    real life; shopping lists, grime
    or microwaves.
It's no good referring back.

But I stand on this verge awaiting half-lights,
A lifeboat to my ditched trawler in the gale.
My catch leaps in the knotted nets at the side,
Even if I could balance along the deck, spirit
Stars or sheer muscle might give way tonight,

here,

    where the breath begins,   oracular

    where sagas of boats and invasions and history's lessons
(so long ignored) are accessed, *for blessed are the peacemakers*

who open the door. I've travelled far
over rock and cliff, fiscal nightmares

    have invested more than monies,

    more than   time.

Mashiga! She's back.

    She squawks her insults, I run down the path –

there is no fence.

I knock –

it's all Millais and lanterns and the passing bells,

    there is rhyme and music and the haunting duduk
carries the lost paradise of words,

    what they emit,
the building,
        humble tenement

where there is a dance of history, a serenade
where Ahab and Ishmael are one and pro pacem,

    the song you sing
        the beat you played
            the line you made
                the breath you gave.

V

Future Haunting

On the other side of your wall
words are encrypted and screamed,
shake partitions, induce tears
that drench your floor, threatens
heat stress to silence.

On the other side of your door
keys to unlock are lost,
your bolts rust unnoticed,
the glazing frosted in the frame.
Your clock is close to midnight.

On the other side of your world
storms collide as ice-walls crumble.
Crop blights mask top soil, so
no soil, no foot or paw prints near.
Your internet blinks in the thunder-wave.

On the other side of your screens
your every image is an electron fog
as tectonic plates shake the ground.
Even your bitcoins create carbon infusions.
I am flood and wildfire, coming closer.

Imagining Stonehouse

i.m. Stephen Laignel

I

kalpas
configured
such is here

such time
such lifting
packing together

the water-wheel turns
a ramshackle strainer
for mountain rice

II

for forty years
I gather wild mushrooms
on this mountain side

gibbons howl
as the tiger laughs
as silverfish

consume my books
such matters
now

III

what appears? fields
grow emerald with or
without me

by Sky Lake
rushes a music
to my waking day

clouds pass below
so dense I cannot channel
water across the slope

IV

I carve this Buddha from clay
my paper window
rustles in the storm

I thatch Shan-Shi
three rafters wide
ten feet inside

who is Shiwu
a moon
sees a finger pointing

V

to hold a simple flower
to smile without reserve
to find a flag

chop down its pole
Ragorata: Anobotei
I sit without end

I gather pigweed
tend my millet
wheat and fragrant rice

VI

I scatter flowers
mash fresh ginger
trim my hibiscus hedge

as squirrels scamper
cranes bend their necks
around pine and plum trees

nearby two streams of tears
one hundred and eighty-
four pebbles beside

VII

you are thoughts that pass by
as cars upon a distant bridge
like clouds across blue skies

I haul my wood to market
let my brush fly
nothing to do or change

to let go in all directions
ten thousand cares dissolve
when you are still

Stonehouse

Endangered Species

prompted by Franz Marc's
'The Fate of the Animals' (1913)

Blue deer fly past swine baying
beyond woodlands, *Der Blaue Reiter*
drowns in *la terre charnelle*.
The fox twists in strident scarlet,
orange spear-bursts highlight shadow forms.
In burnt umber a monumental trunk
like Pisa's tower falls forever.

Wolves gather. Around us
hooves thunder and we are lost, close
to the approaching flames,
stabbed by spikes, snared by tendrils.
Bone shards buff up each mud-bank,
craters multiply *pour la patrie*
by those bloodied at Verdun
who scream in Kabul,
crushed rubble beneath Mariupol.

Different home fires appear
with no hearths for comfort.
We repeat never to be forgotten refrains,
trapped in our own trenches,
colour-blind to each new fracas
seen through a prism energised
in headlines and shrapnel,
lost to drones,
to rigor mortis.

The Thatched Barn

prompted by Samuel Palmer's
'A Barn with a Mossy Roof' (1828/9)

The poor gleaners of Kent scavenged fields,
crusted out some kind of living,
collected the leftovers
modern farming methods did not gather. Then
by cold and candlelight, wrote letters
signed *Swing*
and burnt barns.

> *Some moss clumps charred darker,*
> *others a brighter orange.*
> *Shadows sneak on a crumpled roof as*
> *grassy yellows bunch and sidle up the barn.*
> *A stone wall beside, a distance to a town.*

To secure a full store, timbered doors
are locked until evening when bolts are broken,
home's hunger cries inflame,
raise their rage.

> *Logs become weathered, yield a lonely decay*
> *in crimson and chestnut tones*
> *beneath a white cloud-caked sky.*

Today's forgotten gleaners far from home
also need ends to meet,
still lost as the Adur flows by indifferent
to lost letters, distant families
and the exclusions of history.

From the Quaker Graveyard in Idle

I

Yewdell gave the ground by Westfield Lane
made from callimanco and yeomanry,
founded around clothiers who felt
fitt to have occation
for redemption
and a right to be here.

Walled and fenced out of Windhill and Guiseley
they also came from Calverley and Rawdon
to pay penalties for sitting
on these stone seats in silence,
it being *conveyed for five thousand years*
to be steadfast here and hereabouts.

Each conventicle on this *parcel of land*
penalised; Denbighs and Bowmers fined;
James Marshall robbed six times by Courts;
but better *to dig and delve*,
without vanity or memorial stones.
Wind lives longer than dogma.

They gathered from all over: Greengates,
Bingley, Eccleshill and Bradford.
Fathers, mothers, Friends like Ben Swaine,
lightning would strike within again,
ward off sufferings and the cold outside,
all mixed with this earth.

II

Now overgrown, around twenty-five strides by twenty,
grass blades taller than a toddler
in random bunches. Space left
for litter blown from the road, or, maybe,
from an evening's hang-out by The Privateer
or just caught and catapulted into space
where rocks were hewn from moorland ground.
Here, perhaps, Will or Jonas laboured to make
this gritstone rectangle,
this graveyard Meeting place
and heard Ministry and mourning. Today
we take the drop in the road
pass the noumenal and directions to Shipley
to come to the here and light of it,
where old Quakers would rise and speak
their voices echo around Airedale.
Fewer houses here, then
you could see across the valley to the green peaks
where wind would knife
the knee-joints still pained from Carr Lane skids,
a relentless blow through Westfield.
We consider shelter
as afternoon clouds gather grey.
We do not doff our hats. We bend, finally,
into the wind as it pierces us alive
and pushes us back up,
back to Wrose and beer.

III

Despite geography, I never leave this place
where faces, like history on wheels, flash by
until thoughts break to hold,
return again to a place
where peace is neither the absence of violence
nor sound on mute
but all is contained
as in an open meeting on open ground
open to the wild
and holding fast.

After All Hallows

after Louise Gluck

Still uplands fold away at twilight.
Children lock eyes, lost and lit
beneath Samhain lanterns, their breath
steams over darkening hills
where ley lines criss-cross over rocks.

Without co-ordinates, shelter
beneath the Tor gives relief, for
the ancient way is blocked
in moss-covered paths
hidden under starlight.

No tricks, masks or bonfires
ward them off. The shadows lurk.
Some politician's daughter leans out the window,
her time to bleed. Air stifles the soul:

My children, hear my voice,
see my tears.

And, all in white,
a host off the hills
with pumpkin eyes aflame
creep closer.

Moor Haunts

Even when its light, the crows' calls suggest the ominous,
black-robed their clouding of the day.
A kestrel hovers to hunt, scopes while
white arse-bobbing conies hop off
until snares cut crimson stripes.

Like stags, their tread goes through every under-hoofed
bit of bogland and hollow but without trace,
even though the peat is sodden through.
A fox slinks across the green uphill,
grins blood-drip.

The grey cumulus curtain pulls across the sky
to an ever-darker grey and thickening black.
The wind drives on, bites into trees bending
in the howl,
the howl that aches for rest.

Sand and gritstone boulders rooted near
old lead workings by dampened tracks, laid flat
by the boots of many carrying scran,
axes, picks and shovels over crags
and purple-rich heather.

Water courses through so many channels as we sludge
towards the snickets that await us
where shadows strangely flail and fade
after the sheep's skull. A curlew's cry
bids an eerie farewell.

Quell the Storm

for Reuben

Now beyond you, Coriolis,
this spatial scale by hill and ling
bursts fast-moaning

while I, Aeolian, like the songs,
remain on land to form fertile soils
beyond measure, renewable.

You peel off roofs,
fell trees over roadways.
You scream at me, *Prevail*.

As we twist our meanings
the sky cracks clouds
dazzles sheets of light

amidst our dark longings.
I choose a middle way,
breeze wistfully along the shore.

Where or when to meet?
Only in a tenderness
that once was,

blasted
by a power source
beyond our understanding.

Fitfully we listen,
take shelter,
send our codes for reassurance.

There is a recovery in this,
some rebuilding. If not a forgetting –
a forgiving.

A Still Passing

... sit there like Buddhas in the snow.
– Robert MacFarlane

We look skyward, hush is pressured
on an exposed backdrop, a slow climb.
Rock face a hair's breadth away, hammer holes
and above, an overhang. Out of thick cloud quiet

a shadow form is spotted. A silhouette,
ghost or a barely recalled cairn
unmapped with a point to prove.
The heart beats under random rock falls.

Sight is key but retinas pop at altitude,
silence deepens, *cirrus scarves* or
an omnipresence?
It haunts us. We jam up the crevasse,

oxygen lack conjures strange and brooding images.
He sits, as we pass by, upright against a rock,
eye sockets frosted, hands caked
in cable and white flake.

Above this frozen Buddha we summit.
Peaks pierce the white canopy,
a world below. We catch our breath, quietus,
this unexpected find.

VI

Where Hart's Tongue Dwells

Ice gorged out this land space, each shingle piece
a word in a cairn to last like rocks and seas.

So many rocks and seas your rope saved me from
Predator, Overshadow, Clubfoot and Obsession.

Time rushes like water, coral river swells, fountains
by 400 stone steps carved around Malham

where your word-tide led me to holy fern, hart's tongue,
buckler fern and the remnants of ancient fish bone.

To walk above the grikes, shuffle over the pavement part
with a flicker of magic, or a pearl beyond price, to start

to grow rare as baneberry from those limestone cracks,
to be stronger, incant the spells to redeem my lacks.

For you it wasn't just belay and hard grade climbs,
it was the essence of being, to flow beyond time.

Kufaniya

We return home like weeds on a path,
keep eyes front so not to see
The Watcher, whose glare burns homes,
whose words binds us.
Each child has shards of steel
to machete their dreams
in his way.

We live in blackness. Hawks grab prey,
talons dart sharp as cameras flash
on invited crowds huddling around
The One, whose portrait dominates.
Here a shredded uniform, small
as a child, an inconsequential statistic
for his truth.

The hawks wing to bright facades
where The Beautiful party,
while others as weeds are composted.
We fear our footfall leaves traces, so we,
plucked as lost children, beyond sight
like inconvenient news, emigres
for his profit.

Rebekahs at the Gate

*And they blessed Rebekah and said unto her,
thou art our sister, be thou the mother of thousands
of millions, and let thy seed possess the gate…*
– Genesis 24:60

When all has been taken, pride leaks
like busted gutters, sobs at night
with your wife, hunger pangs
for your sons and daughters.
Your charcoaled face
illuminates every tax break toll-gate
as oil prices rise, harvests fail
and food for the few means
you stampede loudly.
Strangely dressed, your skirts scrape
mown grasses, sods of the earth,
skeletal and proud in white gowns,
despite dignity gone, why not
dress for this occasion?
Better to make a mark Twm,
your *petticoat ghost* will be heard,
perhaps even today we hear
Merched Becca, for the many,
your seed will guard the gate.

Elpis, Daily

In your absence love remains
as close as breath, constant
as space around your chair;
your dinner plate is waiting,
I keep it clean
for your return.

The Ornadels

after Jorge-Luis Borges

I know nothing of the Ornadels,
a Jewish absence, mulched with others,
a line of ghosts anonymous in open trenches;
a mystery of Warsaw ghettoes, rural shadows.
Given how White Cossacks fired border villages
and later ravages, they are unrecorded
strangers indecipherable to the present
and to the process of poetry and art.
Like many, they are buried in earth and oblivion.
Better so? As the famous *untermensch*,
they are the vanguard for the exiles before us,
who leak from scorched lands
to deflating dinghies
or float as flotsam in sea waters.
Maybe there is a mystic Davidic promise
that home can be where you land,
where giants, no matter how imposing,
can be defeated.

Kath Comes Home

Alone, restless at night,
a storm strikes, images
that pain like pins pierce
my insides, as wedges
to force my eyelids open –
a moor-floater from as far off as Clay Cross,
or crag-scrambler down from Lord's Rake.
After each door creak,
an anxiety. A curtain-flap
jolts me awake but
is that sudden snap a lock?
A window rattle when lightning strikes, then
a shout, a high-pitched name-crier.
I rush to the shaken window, cracked
diagonal in this wind-slapped brew.
Impossible to block the shock
but never wanting this to stop
as the eye in the legend of you
meets mine.

Musica Reservata

*in appreciation of John Beckett, Jantina Noorman,
David Munrow and Michael Morrow*

We gather, a motley collection off the streets,
the stage fills to begin the journey;
first stop voices, a musica secreta,
a motet, then *Calenda Maya* announces,
in simple dress, a grey-haired singer
to steer us.

Dinner-suited men in jazz-bright socks
make crumhorns buzz. Her soprano with others
contrasts tones, textures. Nakers demiquaver beat,
a snake, lacquered black as ebony,
increases the volume to herald the next point,
estampie.

Byrd and Des Pres mass voices,
the bespectacled mezzo is transformed,
she embodies an angelic host,
a silver amulet of sound where light dwells
and shadows tell of pain,
of loss, with a consort's consolation.

Minor chords slow us into De Lassus chanson.
A clash of brass and cymbal brings the feast
in rural green, after the working day,
best bib-and-tucker for the Bransle circle,
our hands join as we dance breathlessly
together, thrill at canario and coranto.

Now chromatic, a lute plucks at lost love,
if only she would notice Dowland's melancholy,
his becomes my bereft heart in violet,
a mood in maroon shades to a softer tone,
we relish as connoisseurs the exquisite,
an ars subtilior.

Madrigals delight, we are lit up,
a sound painting, applaud the encore.
Jantina turns, our heartbeat stills,
she stands back while they all bow
and we return to the evening streets
infused with song.

The Long Walk Home

Walking grass-brushed, hare-bells
sway purple in the wind,
a wilderness of peat and bilberry
grit and grounded in rock
sprayed by Low and High Force.
By Cauldron Snout the doomsayer
warns, *If you press on to the fall,*
for fall there is, fear follows.

Scrambles sting the knee,
how distances amass memories
ten thousand paces today,
up hills to white foam
shoots over Crow's Stones
millennia in the making.
South Tees washes miles,
while bees dance pollen in the sun.

Cairn Hill is a hard-breath climb,
forget Orgreave? It is Tina's crew
who market our children's silver
to pocket gold. This earth cannot be bought
or sold. We are the carers for sundew
and starred bog asphodel. Nurture
this England, as a child in your arms,
for all our tomorrows.

Emerson's Tonic

Live in the sunshine,
swim the sea, drink the wild air...
– Ralph Waldo Emerson

For just ten minutes in its entire life
a pear tastes at its best, its flesh
liquid and succulent. In that same time
you arrive somewhere the path divides.
Which way to go? Onward, to the far hills?
Or back to a townscape of familiar streets?

The dilemma, like being peeled, reveals
flesh that will ripen or bruise beneath the sun.
To prepare, sample the rich juice, savour
the wild air. Will a strength be honed
to pave a better path?

Notes & Acknowledgements

'C'mon Town!' – The epigraph is from a speech by Frederick Douglass on 03.viii.1857, see *Selected Speeches and Writings*, p.vi; other sources give: West India Emancipation Speech, delivered at Canandaigua, New York (04.viii.1857), see *The Life and Writings of Frederick Douglass*, p.437 (Philip S. Foner ed., 1950). Halifax Town's home ground is The Shay. The old home fans stand is called the Skircoat, whose entrance is via Hunger Hill.

'Companionship' – the italicised phrase is from Anna Akhmatova's 'Little Songs 4: Love Song', see her *Selected Poems* (Newcastle, 1989) p.211.

'Watercress In Kearsney' – written for the Kearsney Abbey site Dover Arts Development project featuring poetry, art and film led by the D.A.D. Officer, Joanna Jones.

'Classifying 'Together'' – I associate the phrase "unity in varieties" with William Blake but Waldo Emerson also asserts this as part of his Nature essay (Section V: Discipline), see *Essential Writings of Ralph Waldo Emerson*; ed. Brooks Anderson, introduction by Mary Oliver (New York, 2000), p.22.

'John Milton's Contention' – In November 1644 John Milton wrote in his *Areopagitica*: "I cannot praise a fugitive and cloistered virtue, unexercised and unbreathed, that never sallies out and sees her adversary, but slinks out of the race where that immortal garland is to be run for, not without dust and heat."

'A Dance That Will Not Die' – see *Way of the Morris*: a documentary film by Tim Plester (2009).

'Monument To The Red Soilers' – Magpie Mine's history spans more than 200 years of bonanzas and failures, of bitter disputes and fights resulting in the 1833 "murder" of three Maypitt miners in the running dispute with the Magpie Miners who both worked the Great Redsoil Vein. The Widows' Curse is said to remain to this day.

'The Second Flaming' – Tony Benn spoke about each generation having to repeat the struggle for real democracy and that each generation's work is spurred on by two flames: one of anger at injustice, one the flame of hope. The poem was short-listed in the 2016 Rebellion Save As Competition.

'The Singer' – Henry Hevingham's poem 'If music be the food of love' was set to music by Purcell. Hearing Rowan Pierce's interpretation was a prompt. The last line of the first stanza is taken from the poem and the second line of the second stanza references it. The line "all things made good" was quoted (variant of Romans 8:28?) in Lachlan Mackinnon's poem 'The Psalmist' from which this poem is a reaction.

'Night Lines' – This poem was prompted by Jeremy Mann's image *Construction* (2011) and presented to me by Gary Studley in a session of SoundLines, an East Kent group of poets.

'There Are Two St. Augustines, Matt' – I stumbled on James J. O'Donnell's biography of Augustine of Hippo [*Augustine the African*] which has informed the poem for which I offer my thanks. Words in italics come from Augustine of Hippo's *Confessions*.

'Concert In Yarmouk' – see *The Pianist of Yarmouk* by Aeham Ahmad (London, 2019). This was short-listed for the Bridport Poetry Prize, 2021.

'Scree At Pendle Hill' – The quotation ("Be valiant…") is from George Fox, founder of the Religious Society of Friends, see: Para. 19:32 in *Quaker faith and practice; Yearly Meeting of the Religious Society of Friends*, 3rd ed, (London, 1995, 2005).

'Sketches of John Clare' – The italics relate to poem titles except "Kop, kop" which comes from Clare's poem 'The Hoars Frost Lodges in Every Tree'; "A distance from the town" is a line in 'Song (The Rain Is Come)' and used as a title by Gordon Tyrrall for his excellent CD airing his take on Clare's music and poetry. The poem can be found in *Major Works*, ed.'s Eric Robinson & David Powell (Oxford, 1984, 2004), p.381; the others come from *John Clare By Himself*, ed.'s Eric Robinson & David Powell (Manchester, 1996, 2002). Despite the academic controversy, I would acknowledge the debt I owe to Eric Robinson for his devotion to the work of John Clare.

'Cold And Shallow Waters' – The first two lines of the second stanza are an adaptation from 'Ghazal (V) of the Dead Child', see *Selected Poems, Federico Garcia Lorca*; ed. Christopher Maurer (London, 1997) p.243.

'Trying To Find Charles Olson's House' was runner-up in a Summer Poetry Kit Competition. The phrases "bending the bow" and "the form of women" echo titles by Robert Duncan and Robert Creeley respectively. "We pour out like water" borrows a line from Robert Lowell's 'From the Quaker Graveyard in Nantucket', and "red wheelbarrows", iconically, from William Carlos Williams. Like 'On Dungeness Beach' and 'The Long Walk Home', this was included in my previous book (*Breath-Taking: A Geography*, Lapwing 2016) but needed to be revisited.

'Future Haunting' – For "heat stress", see *The Uninhabitable Earth: a story for the future*; David Wallace-Wells, (London, 2019), p.40.

'Imagining Stonehouse' – Prompted by Red Pine's translation of the poems/talks of *Stonehouse or Shiwu* (Berkeley, 1999; pp.127,131) and his *Teachings of Bodhidharma* (Washington, 1987, pp.73, 99). I am grateful to have found 'Shan-Shih: the hermit house of Stonehouse' on the internet. Some elements have been prompted by the teachings of Dogen Zenji's Shobogenzo: 'Genjo-Koan' (The Problem of Everyday Life) from *Zen Is Eternal Life*; by Roshi P.T.N.H. Jiyu-Kennett; Shasta Abbey Press(1999), 4th ed. pp.228, 231, 253, 269, 270, 286.

'Endangered Species' – "Der Blaue Reiter" was the name of the artistic group co-founded by Franz Marc. "La terre charnelle" and "pour la patrie" echo phrases used by Geoffrey Hill in his *The Mystery of the Charity of Charles Peguy* – see his *Broken Hierarchies: Poems 1952-2012*, Kenneth Haynes (ed); (Oxford, 2013), pp. 147, 150.

'Winter Journey' – prompted by Friedrich's *Winter Landscape* (circa. 1810). Caspar David encouraged his brother Johann, it is thought, to go ice-skating with him. Tragically Johann fatally fell through the ice on the frozen lake. Some reports suggest Johann was trying to save Caspar David. *Sea of Ice* is one of his paintings, 'The Good Old Way' is a Victorian hymn recorded by The Watersons on *For Pence and Spicy Ale* (Topic, 1975).

'From The Quaker Graveyard In Idle' – The quotations are from J. Horsfall Turner's *Idle Upper Chapel Burial Registers and Graveyard Inscriptions* (1906). Perhaps, the last Quaker Meeting held there was in 1905. The Jonas in the poem was one Jonas Adcock, a callimanco maker from Idle, the Will was William Hustler of Bradford.

'Quell the Storm' – The Coriolis Effect, named after French mathematician/physicist Gaspard-Gustave de Coriolis, is the process which makes things (like planes or currents of air) travelling long distances around the Earth seem to move at a curve as opposed to a straight line.

'A Still Passing' – "They sit there like Buddhas in the snow"; "Sight is often all you have at high altitudes." The summit of Pik Pobeda: Victory Peak in the Tian Shan mountains. *Mountains of the Mind: a history of a fascination*; Robert MacFarlane (London 2003), pp.137–138.

'Where Hart's Tongue Dwells' – Clubfoot, Overshadow, Obsession and Predator are particularly hard rock climbs around Malham. Steve McClure's was the first ascent of Overshadow (9a). Jericho Brown's Duplex poem structure kindled this "variant" of it.

'Kufaniya' – The title references Anjan Sundaram's *Bad News: Last Journalists in a Dictatorship* (London, 2016). This Rwandan word, according to Anjan Sundaram, relates to a Presidential policy of killing the government's own troops and use of child soldiers for which "only several warlords have been prosecuted" (p.143).

'The Ornadels' and 'After All Hallows' were prompted and framed by Jorge-Luis Borges's poem entitled 'The Borges' and Louise Gluck's poem 'All Hallows'.

'Rebekahs At The Gate' – Twm Carnabwth, the accepted leader of the first protests, wore women's clothes when leading attacks. The phrase "petticoat ghosts" comes from 'Newtown Jericho' by The Alarm; "for the many" references Shelley's *The Masque of Anarchy* recently taken up in Labour Party manifestos.

'Emerson's Tonic' – Ralph Waldo Emerson (1803–1882) asserted that pears were at their best for only 10 minutes. The epigram is from his poem 'Merlin's Song' – see *Essential Writings of Ralph Waldo Emerson*; ed. Brooks Anderson, introduction by Mary Oliver (New York, 2000), pp.732–733.